High-Interest/Low-Readability Nonfiction

Wild Animals

by Kathryn Wheeler

Carson-Dellosa Publishing Company, Inc.
Greensboro, North Carolina

Credits

Editor:
Ashley Anderson

Layout Design:
Van Harris

Inside Illustrations:
Donald O'Connor

Cover Design:
Annette Hollister-Papp
Peggy Jackson

Cover Illustration:
Tara Tavonatti

The Huge Hunter

If you were planning to hunt for food in the coldest place on earth, how would you get ready? Probably by dressing very warmly! The **polar bear** is always "dressed" for its constant hunt for meat. The polar bear is covered with fur. Even the bottoms of its feet have fur on them. Its huge claws dig into the snow so that it can run without slipping. But, that's just the start of the polar bear's winter wear.

The polar bear has a thick layer of fat to keep it warm. This layer can be more than four inches thick. Its skin is black. Black is the best color to hold in the sun's warmth. Why doesn't the polar bear's white fur reflect the sun? Because even its fur is designed to keep the bear warm. Here's a surprise: the polar bear does not have white fur! The fur only looks white because of the sun's reflection. Polar bear fur is clear. Each hair is hollow. The sun travels through the fur and into the bear's black skin. This system is so good that the bear cannot be seen at all in infrared photos, pictures of things that give off heat. The bear's body traps heat well.

The polar bear hunts on the snow and in the water. The bear's feet are webbed to help it swim. It is a good diver and can see underwater. On the ice, the polar bear can be patient and still. The polar bear looks for an airhole that a seal has made in the ice. It can wait beside one of these holes for hours without moving. When the seal pokes its nose up to breathe, the bear grabs it and pulls it onto the ice. Seal meat makes up the largest part of the bear's diet. But, something is happening to make it harder for polar bears to hunt.

? Make a prediction.
What do you think the author will write about next? Circle your answer.

polar bear hibernation   polar bear cubs   polar bear hunting problems

Conversion
4 inches = 10.16 centimeters

Next Page →

© Carson-Dellosa

CD-104178 ▪ Wild Animals   **37**

Printed in the USA • All rights reserved.

ISBN 1-59441-318-5

Table of Contents

Introduction

Struggling readers in the upper-elementary and middle grades face a difficult challenge. While many of their peers are reading fluently, they are still working to acquire vocabulary and comprehension skills. They face a labyrinth of standardized tests, which can be a nightmare for struggling readers. And, they face another major difficulty—the challenge of remaining engaged and interested while working to improve reading skills.

High-Interest/Low-Readability Nonfiction: Wild Animals can help! All of the articles in this book are written at a fourth-grade reading level with an interest level from grade 4 to adult.

Throughout the book, the stories use repeated vocabulary to help students acquire and practice new words. The stories are crafted to grab students' attention while honing specific reading skills, such as uncovering author's purpose; defining vocabulary; making predictions; and identifying details, synonyms, antonyms, and figures of speech. Most of the comprehension questions parallel standardized-test formats so that students can become familiar with the structure without the pressure of a testing situation. And, the articles even utilize the familiar "Next Page" arrows and "Stop" signs seen in most standardized tests. The questions also include short-answer formats for writing practice.

Best of all, this book will build confidence in students as they learn that reading is fun, enjoyable, and fascinating!

Note: Stories that include measurements, such as an animal's height or weight, also feature a convenient conversion box with measurements rounded to the nearest hundredth. Students will find this useful as they become familiar with converting standard and metric measurements. If students are not currently studying measurement conversion, simply instruct them to ignore the box. Or, cover it when making copies of a story.

Weeks without Water

How long could you live without water? Scientists say that you could not live more than two or three days. But, if you were an **oryx**, you could live for weeks without a drink of water! This fast-running animal lives in a hot, dusty world. So, it's a good thing that it hardly ever needs to drink.

The oryx looks a little like a big deer or an antelope. It lives in Africa. The oryx likes to live in a large herd of about 50 to 60 animals. But, the herd splits apart to look for shade trees. The oryx seeks out any shade it can find. This keeps it safe from the blazing sun.

How does the oryx go so long without drinking water? It gets up early! The oryx eats grass that still has dew on it. The wet grass of the early morning has enough water on it to keep the oryx alive.

The oryx lives with danger. One enemy is the lion. Lions like to eat oryx meat. But, sometimes a hungry lion gets a bad shock. The oryx has two long, straight horns. It can use its horns like spears. As a lion runs at a cornered oryx, the oryx lowers its head. Sometimes, it can kill the lion using its horns.

Are the oryx and the lion always enemies? Not if you know about a story from 2002. A lioness found a baby oryx alone. Its mother had gone to find food. The lioness did not eat the baby. Instead, she adopted the little oryx on the spot! She took care of it for two weeks. Sadly, one day the lioness was asleep. A male lion came near. He killed the baby before the new mother woke up. It was the end of this strange story of enemies turning into family members. It shows that nature always has surprises for us.

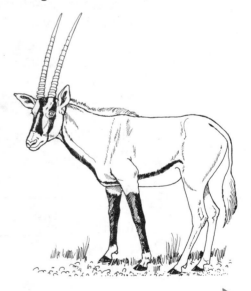

Next Page

Weeks without Water

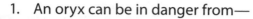

Answer the questions below.

1. An oryx can be in danger from—
   a. an antelope.
   b. a deer.
   c. a lion.
   d. an eagle.

2. Read the following sentence from the story and answer the question.

   The oryx eats grass that still has dew on it.

   What is *dew*?
   a. beads of water
   b. rain
   c. sap
   d. insects

3. Circle two adjectives that tell about the oryx.

   fast   huge   small

   slow   horned   spotted

4. Finish this sentence about a story from 2002.

   A _____

   found a baby _____

   alone and _____

   _____ .

5. What is one feature of the oryx?
   a. It can go for weeks without drinking water.
   b. It has long, straight horns.
   c. It can run very fast.
   d. all of the above

6. Read the following sentence from the story and answer the question.

   The oryx likes to live in a large herd of about 50 to 60 animals.

   What is another word for *herd*?
   a. river
   b. group
   c. trio
   d. pair

7. How does the oryx use its horns to protect itself?

   It uses its horns like

   _____ .

Biggest Bill on the Block

Have you seen pictures of a **toucan**? It is a hard bird to miss! It has a huge yellow, orange, and black bill that makes up one-third of its body. Some toucans have green and red in their bills, too. With a bill that big, why doesn't the toucan tip over? Because the bill is light in weight. It is hollow and feels like a dry sponge. The bill has "teeth" built into the edges. The teeth let the toucan eat many different foods: fruit, tree frogs, small snakes, and other birds' eggs!

But, why does the toucan's bill have to be so big? Scientists can't agree on an answer. Some think that the toucan's big bill scares away enemies. Some think that it helps the bird get food from the ends of branches. Other scientists say that the huge bill has no real use at all.

The toucan also has other strange features, like its feet. Think about what it would be like to have toes growing out of your heels! That's what the toucan has. It has two toes that face forward and two that face backward. This helps the bird keep a tight grip on wet branches in the rain forest.

The other interesting thing about the toucan is its "feather" tongue. The bird has *bristles*, or sharp, little hairs, on the end of its tongue. They help the bird make its loud, croaking call. In the rain forest, you can hear a toucan that is far away!

Toucans are friendly birds. In the rain forest, they live in flocks of six or more birds. They look for homes in hollow trees. Then, they all sleep together in one big nest inside the tree. When toucans have babies, both the mother and father sit on the eggs and feed the chicks. The toucan's friendly nature makes it easy to tame when it lives in a zoo.

Next Page

Biggest Bill on the Block

Answer the questions below.

1. What is one of the toucan's most interesting features?
   a. its small bill
   b. its soft, lovely song
   c. its five-toed feet
   d. none of the above

2. Read the following sentence from the story and answer the question.

   It has a huge yellow, orange, and black bill that makes up one-third of its body.

   What is another word for *bill*?
   a. wing
   b. head
   c. toe
   d. beak

3. Choose the BEST description of the toucan.
   a. a friendly bird with funny feet
   b. a large-billed rain forest bird that lives in groups
   c. a small, black bird that eats leaves
   d. a rain forest bird

4. What are *bristles*? Write your answer in a complete sentence.

   _____

   _____

   _____

5. Write three words or phrases from the story that tell about the toucan's bill.

   a. _____

   _____

   b. _____

   _____

   c. _____

   _____

6. Which of these is a reason that scientists give for the toucan having such a big bill?
   a. It may be used to send messages to other toucans.
   b. It may help the toucan get food from the ends of branches.
   c. It may help the toucan take care of its babies.
   d. It may help the toucan climb trees.

7. Circle three adjectives that describe the toucan.

   slow   friendly   loud

   big-billed   meat-eating   fierce

The Egg-Laying Mammal

When people in England first saw a stuffed **platypus**, they thought it was a joke. They thought someone had put a duck's bill on a beaver's body! Then, they saw other strange things. The platypus had webbed feet. It had short legs like a lizard. It had two layers of fur. And, it had a *spur* on its back leg. What kind of animal was this?

The platypus lives in Australia. It is one of the strangest animals in the world. For one thing, it lays eggs, even though it is a mammal. It lives underground, but it spends a lot of time in the water. A platypus dives in the water up to 80 times an hour to get food. Its webbed feet and flat tail help it swim. It catches worms, snails, and shrimp deep in ponds and streams. It carries food in pouches in its cheeks until it is ready to eat. The platypus does not have teeth. Instead, it has little pads inside its bill that grind up its food.

This furry brown animal is about the size of a house cat. It lives about as long as a cat, too—10 to 17 years. Its babies are called *puggles*. They hatch out of their eggs and then the mother platypus feeds them milk. The babies live in *burrows*, or underground nests that are built with long tunnels for doorways. Platypuses like to make burrows on the banks of rivers or streams. This lets them hunt for food easily.

Only the male platypus has a spur that it uses like a stinger. It uses the spur in fighting. When another animal is stung, it can die. Humans do not die from the sting of a platypus. But, they do get very sick. The poison in a spur causes great pain. No medicine can make it better. Settlers in Australia quickly learned to leave this shy, funny-looking animal alone!

Next Page

The Egg-Laying Mammal

Answer the questions below.

1. Read the following sentence from the story and answer the question.

   Platypuses like to make burrows on the banks of rivers or streams.

   Which definition of the word *banks* matches the way it is used in the sentence from the story?
   a. places to keep money
   b. sets of cards or chips used in games
   c. groups of clouds
   d. sloped ground on the edge of a body of water

2. What is a *puggle*? Write your answer in a complete sentence.

   _____

   _____

   _____

3. Which of the following is NOT a feature of the platypus?
   a. a bill like a duck's
   b. a flat tail like a beaver's
   c. paws like a dog's
   d. short legs like a lizard's

4.–8. Write T for true and F for false.

4. _____ The platypus carries its babies in a pouch.

5. _____ The platypus is shy.

6. _____ The platypus lays eggs.

7. _____ Only the female platypus can sting someone.

8. _____ The platypus dives up to 10 times an hour for food.

9. Choose the word that BEST completes this sentence:

   The platypus carries poison in its _____ .

   a. stinger
   b. spur
   c. pouch
   d. claw

10. Instead of teeth, the platypus has

    _____

    inside its _____

    that grind up its _____ .

STOP

Gentle Giants

Imagine having a six-foot-long neck! Now, imagine that your legs are six feet long, too. That would make you the tallest animal on the planet. Welcome to the world of the **giraffe**.

Why is the giraffe so tall? Its long legs and long neck let it eat leaves from the tops of trees. The giraffe uses its 18-inch-long black tongue to help it pull leaves off trees. This animal giant spends at least half of each day eating. It can only eat a few leaves at a time. And, because it is so big, it eats about 75 pounds of food a day. That's a lot of chewing!

Because adult giraffes are so big, they don't have many enemies. But, baby giraffes do. Meat-eating animals like lions try to kill the babies. Luckily, mother giraffes have a system to guard their babies. They use baby-sitters. One giraffe looks after a whole group of babies. The other mothers go off to eat. If a lion comes close, the baby-sitter will kick it away. A kick from a six-foot-long leg must hurt!

When giraffes drink, they bend their heads low. A crocodile might try to bite them as they do this. So, giraffes work together to get water, too. They go to a pond in a group. One giraffe acts as the guard while the others drink water.

These gentle animals always travel in their *herds*, or groups. When you see them on the African plain, sometimes they look like they are alone, but they aren't. Because a giraffe is so tall, it can see over half of a mile away. As long as it can see the other animals in its family, it feels safe. The giraffes will moo, hiss, and whistle to "talk" to each other as they eat.

Conversions

6 feet = 1.83 meters
18 inches = 45.72 centimeters
75 pounds = 34.02 kilograms
0.5 mile = 0.8 kilometers

Next Page

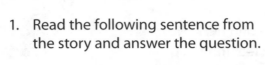

Gentle Giants

Answer the questions below.

1. Read the following sentence from the story and answer the question.

   This animal giant spends at least half of each day eating.

   Why does the giraffe spend so much time eating?

   a. It likes to eat strange foods.
   b. It is so big that it needs a lot of food.
   c. It has to find food for its babies.
   d. Its neck is so long.

2. Which of the following is a feature of the giraffe?

   a. 18-inch-long legs
   b. a red tongue
   c. a six-foot-long tail
   d. six-foot-long legs

3. Giraffe mothers use a

   _____

   to guard their babies.

4. _____ might attack

   giraffes when they drink.

5. The giraffe's _____

   is 18 inches long.

6. Adult giraffes are very tall, so they

   don't have many _____ .

7. What conclusion about giraffes can you draw from the article?

   a. Giraffes like to be on their own.
   b. Giraffes work together as a group in many ways.
   c. Giraffes don't run very fast.
   d. Giraffes are silent animals.

8. Choose the word or words that BEST complete this sentence:

   Giraffes live on the plains of
   _____.

   a. Asia
   b. South America
   c. Australia
   d. Africa

9. A giraffe has special "shut-off" valves in its neck. These keep its blood from rushing to its head when it bends over. Why do you think that this is important?

   a. The giraffe's neck has a lot of blood in it, and the giraffe would faint if all of the blood went to its head at once.
   b. The giraffe would have to run to get its heart working again.
   c. The giraffe would not be able to move its jaws if too much blood went to them.

STOP

Brilliant Bait

Have you ever seen a **clown fish**? You probably have. The clown fish has bright stripes and colors just like a clown. That is probably where it got its name. There are many different patterns and colors on the bodies of clown fish. The most common is orange with white and black stripes.

A real clown fish is not funny. The clown fish is a fierce fish. It protects its home and its eggs with care. The female clown fish lays between 300 and 700 eggs at one time. But, the male clown fish takes care of the eggs. He watches them until they hatch. One strange thing about clown fish is that they can change gender. If a female dies or is killed, the male can change into a female in a few weeks. Then, it mates with a male and keeps laying eggs.

The clown fish has a strange home. It lives in the arms, or *tentacles*, of a sea animal called an **anemone**. These two animals have made a deal with each other. The anemone doesn't eat the clown fish and provides a safe home. In return, the clown fish does three things for the anemone. It cleans the anemone's tentacles, eating leftover bits of food. It guards the anemone against some enemies. And, it acts as bait. The clown fish's bright stripes draw other fish to the deadly tentacles. The anemone stings these fish and eats them. The "friendship" between these two sea animals works very well for both of them.

Where in the world does the clown fish live? It can be found in the seas near India, Indonesia, and Australia. Each bright, strong little fish always lives with the same sea anemone, never leaving its side.

Brilliant Bait

Answer the questions below.

1. How many eggs can a female clown fish lay at one time? Write your answer in a complete sentence.

   _____

   _____

   _____

2. Choose the word that BEST completes this sentence:

   Another word for *tentacles* is _____.

   a. spurs
   b. hands
   c. arms
   d. eyes

3.–7. Write T for true and F for false.

3. _____ The clown fish can change gender.

4. _____ A female clown fish lays 5,000 eggs at a time.

5. _____ Anemones kill clown fish for food.

6. _____ The anemone uses its tentacles to sting fish.

7. _____ All clown fish are orange with white and black stripes.

8. Which of the following does NOT describe the clown fish?

   a. brightly colored
   b. timid
   c. funny
   d. b. and c.

9. Finish the sentences to list the three things that a clown fish does for a sea anemone.

   a. It cleans the anemone's

   _____ .

   b. It guards the anemone against

   _____ .

   c. It acts as _____

   to attract food for the anemone.

10. From where did the clown fish probably get its name? Write your answer in a complete sentence.

   _____

   _____

   _____

   _____

STOP

Don't Move—I Can Hear You!

If you saw a **serval**, you might want to say, "What big ears you have!" This African cat is only about twice the size of a house cat. But, its ears are huge! It also has very long legs. These two features make the serval a great hunter.

The serval likes to hunt in places with tall grass. Because its legs are so long, it can see over the top of the grass. It looks for its *prey*, the animals it is hunting. Sometimes, it scares a bird in the tall grass. Then, it can jump so high and so fast that it can catch the bird as it starts to fly! The serval can jump up to 10 feet in the air.

When it hunts, the serval also listens with its huge ears. A serval can hear very well. It can even hear mice running underground. It quickly digs up a mouse from its tunnel and eats it before it can get away. Servals also eat lizards, frogs, hares, and baby antelopes.

Servals like to live and hunt alone. But, they are also hunted. Some people catch the serval for its fur. This wild cat has yellow or brown fur with black spots. Its chest and stomach are white with black spots or circles. And, its tail has rings, like the tail of a raccoon.

Other servals are caught and sold as pets. This is sad because servals are wild animals. They are cute as kittens but usually grow up to be wild and fierce. Pet owners have to give them up because they can hurt people. Zoos and pet shelters have to try to find new homes for the servals.

Conversion

10 feet = 3.05 meters

Next Page

Don't Move—I Can Hear You!

Answer the questions below.

1. Read the following sentence from the story and answer the question.

   If you saw a serval, you might want to say, "What big ears you have!"

   The quotation in this sentence is from—
   a. *Cinderella.*
   b. *Goldilocks and the Three Bears.*
   c. *Little Red Riding Hood.*
   d. *Hansel and Gretel.*

2. The serval uses its long legs to—
   a. jump into the air to catch birds.
   b. see above tall grass when it is hunting.
   c. jump into trees to look for food.
   d. a. and b.

3. How high can the serval jump?
   a. two feet
   b. five feet
   c. 10 feet
   d. 15 feet

4. Which of the following does the serval NOT eat?
   a. lizards
   b. leaves
   c. frogs
   d. mice

5. The serval is hunted by—
   a. giraffes.
   b. sharks.
   c. humans.
   d. apes.

6. Which of the following BEST states the main idea of this story?
   a. Servals use their long legs to help them hunt.
   b. Servals are best left in the wild.
   c. Servals are fierce, wild cats that are good hunters.
   d. Servals are funny-looking because of their spotted fur.

7. Do you think the serval should be sold as a pet? Why or why not? Write your answer in a complete sentence.

   _____

   _____

   _____

   _____

Conversions
2 feet = 0.61 meters
5 feet = 1.52 meters
10 feet = 3.05 meters
15 feet = 4.57 meters

STOP

Catch Me If You Can!

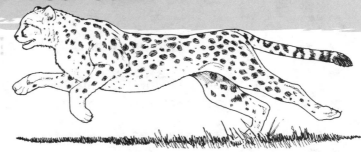

Here's a rule of the African grassland: You can't get eaten if you run really fast. The **cheetah** seems to know this. It is the fastest land animal on Earth. In fact, the cheetah can go from standing still to running 40 miles per hour in just three strides. In seconds, it can be running 70 miles per hour. That's quicker than most cars!

The cheetah's body helps it to run fast. A cheetah has long legs. It has special pads on its paws to keep it from sliding. The cheetah also has extra-large lungs to help it take deep breaths as it races across the ground. Dark marks under its eyes that look like black tears keep the sun from blinding the cheetah. And, this big cat has lightweight bones, too. All of this helps it to run fast. It runs away from enemies, but it also uses its speed to hunt.

The cheetah is a good hunter. But, it has to guard the food it has killed. Bigger animals, like lions, sometimes take the cheetah's meat away from it. If this happens, the cheetah goes hungry that day. It cannot hunt again until the next day because it has to rest after running so fast.

A mother cheetah teaches her babies about running and hunting. She will hurt a small animal and then bring it back to her cubs to chase and kill. She lets them play games to get them to run fast. Cheetahs actually play games that we know. Tag is their favorite. They also love to wrestle. But, the cubs will not be good hunters until they are about three years old.

After the cubs grow up, the females will go off on their own until they have their own babies. Brother cheetahs often stay together for life. They help each other hunt. They pick a *territory*, or land that will be their hunting ground. Then, they defend it together.

Conversions

40 miles per hour = 64.37 kilometers per hour
70 miles per hour = 112.65 kilometers per hour

Catch Me If You Can!

Answer the questions below.

1. Read the following sentences from the story and answer the question.

   In fact, the cheetah can go from standing still to running 40 miles per hour in just three strides. In seconds, it can be running 70 miles per hour. That's quicker than most cars!

   What is the author's purpose in writing these sentences together?

   a. to compare the cheetah's speed with something we know
   b. to describe the cheetah's legs
   c. to tell us that cheetahs are better than cars
   d. all of the above

2. Which of the following sentences about the cheetah is true?

   a. The cheetah is the fastest animal in the universe.
   b. Mother cheetahs and cubs stay together for 10 years.
   c. Cheetah brothers often stay together for life.
   d. Cheetahs can't run very fast because their paws are too big.

3. Which of the following definitions of *territory* is used in the story?

   a. land where cheetahs raise babies
   b. land where cheetahs hunt
   c. land where cheetahs go to die
   d. land where cheetahs wait to be taken to zoos

4. What games do cheetah cubs play?

   a. hide-and-seek
   b. tag
   c. wrestling
   d. b. and c.

5. Why is it important for a cheetah to guard its prey after it is killed?

   a. Bigger animals might take it.
   b. The cheetah will go hungry if the meat is stolen.
   c. The cheetah is too tired to hunt again until the next day.
   d. all of the above

6. How old do cheetahs have to be before they can hunt well?

   _____

7. Why do cheetahs have black marks under their eyes?

   _____

   _____

8. What is one thing that helps the cheetah to run fast?

   _____

   _____

STOP

Quiet, I'm Sleeping

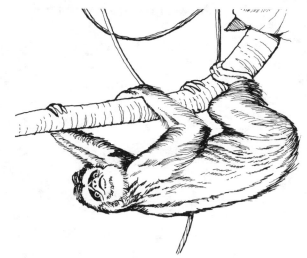

Adult humans sleep about eight hours each night. The **three-toed sloth** sleeps at least twice that long. A sloth needs about 15 to 20 hours of sleep a day. When it wakes up at night, it has a busy life. It eats leaves. Sometimes, it moves slowly to the next tree and eats more leaves. And, sometimes while it is eating, the sloth nods off again!

The sloth is not lazy. Its life of sleep and slow moves lets it save energy. In the rain forest, the sloth sleeps and eats high up in the trees. This keeps it safe from most of its enemies. Large snakes and big birds will sometimes attack the sloth in the trees. Most other animals cannot reach it there. When it comes down to the ground, the sloth is in constant danger. The sloth has long, sharp claws to use if it has to fight. But, it moves very slowly and is easy to catch. Because of this danger, the sloth only climbs down from the treetops about once a week. Sloths do not seem afraid of humans and often live near villages in Central and South America.

Sloths are so still and quiet that for a long time, scientists thought they stayed in one tree for their whole lives! This is not true. The sloth climbs from one tree to another so that it can keep eating leaves.

The sloth spends the rest of its time upside down. It hangs from branches by its feet. The sloth sleeps and eats upside down. Because it spends so much time like this, some of its *organs*—its liver, stomach, and spleen—are in different places than in other animals. This is just one more difference for this strangely different, snoozing animal.

Next Page

Quiet, I'm Sleeping

Answer the questions below.

1.–5. Match each word to its antonym.

1. _____ snoozing   a. defend

2. _____ attack   b. safety

3. _____ upside down c. jungle

4. _____ danger   d. awake

5. _____ villages   e. upright

6. Read the following sentences from the story and answer the question.

   Sometimes, it moves slowly to the next tree and eats more leaves. And, sometimes while it is eating, the sloth nods off again!

   What is a synonym for *nods off*?
   a. agrees
   b. defends
   c. falls asleep
   d. wakes up

7. Look at the word *organs* in the last paragraph of the story. Which of the following definitions matches the way it is used in the story?
   a. musical instruments with keyboards
   b. parts inside a body that perform specific tasks
   c. organizations inside a company, like a newsletter staff
   d. smaller groups in a government

8. Finish these sentences.
   a. The sloth sleeps so much to

      _____.

   b. The sloth spends a lot of its life

      hanging _____

      _____.

   c. Two of the sloth's enemies are

      _____

      _____.

9. Circle the correct word or phrase in parentheses to complete each sentence.

   a. The sloth (**does** , **does not**) seem to be afraid of humans.

   b. The sloth needs to sleep up to (**10** , **20** , **24**) hours a day.

   c. The sloth eats during the (**day** , **night**).

   d. The sloth uses its sharp (**teeth** , **toes** , **claws**) if it needs to fight.

A Golden Good-Bye?

The sailors in Magellan's crew saw the **golden lion tamarin** on their trip around the world. They thought it was a kind of tree-climbing cat with the face of a lion. The tamarin is really from the same family as the monkey. It is about the size of a squirrel, but it has a longer tail. It has red-gold fur and a mane around its face like a lion's. This little animal lives in the rain forest of Brazil.

The tamarin looks for food during the day. It eats fruit, insects, and lizards. Tamarins roam the tops of trees. At night, they sleep in nests in hollow trees. Their biggest enemies are birds, like eagles and hawks. The tamarin has a special call to warn about large birds. Sometimes, a tamarin will drop all the way to the ground to keep a large bird from attacking it. Their other enemies are jungle cats, like *jaguars*, and snakes.

Hawks and jaguars aren't the tamarin's biggest problem. Humans are. People are tearing down the rain forest. They are selling the wood and building farms on the land. Almost 99 percent of the forest where the tamarin lives is gone. Animals like the tamarin have nowhere to go when their homes are lost. In the 1970s, there were only about 200 tamarins left in the world.

Today, the tamarin's home is being kept safe. There are now about 1,000 tamarins in the rain forest. They are watched carefully. The people of Brazil are working to help save this small animal. So are other groups around the world. Maybe the tamarin will not become extinct after all.

A Golden Good-Bye?

Answer the questions below.

1. _____ was an explorer who saw the golden lion tamarin.

2. The tamarin was once thought to be a type of _____, but it belongs to the same family as the _____ .

3. The tamarin gets its name from the _____ around its face that looks like a lion's.

4. Tamarins are afraid of large birds like hawks and _____ .

5. The tamarin is about the size of a _____, but it has a longer _____ .

6.–9. Write T for true and F for false.

6. _____ Today, there are only 200 tamarins left in the world.

7. _____ Tamarins eat leaves and flowers.

8. _____ The tamarin has a special warning call for large birds.

9. _____ All of the forest where the tamarin used to live is gone.

10. Read the following sentence from the story and answer the question.

Tamarins roam the tops of trees.

What is a synonym for *roam*?
a. race
b. wander
c. climb
d. eat

11. Do you think that it is important to save animals like the tamarin? Why or why not? Write your answer in complete sentences.

_____

_____

_____

_____

_____

_____

From the Days of the Dinosaurs

The **tuatara** is special. It is just the same as it was 200 million years ago. It has not *evolved*, or changed. Tuataras used to live with dinosaurs. Now, the tuatara has a different roommate: a bird called a **petrel**.

Petrels are birds that make *burrows*, or tunnel nests, in the sand. The tuatara moves in with the petrel. In some ways, this is a good deal. The petrel goes out during the day to look for food. The tuatara sleeps a lot during the day. It also watches the petrel chicks. But, if the tuatara gets hungry, he might have one of the chicks as a snack! Tuataras also eat insects and worms. Sometimes, it even eats a baby tuatara or two.

Tuataras look like two-foot-long lizards, but they are not lizards. The tuatara is a reptile, but its closest relatives are all extinct. The tuatara is *endangered*, or in danger of becoming extinct. It has teeth that are part of its jaw bone and loose, soft, green skin with scales. And, it has three eyes! The tuatara's third eye gets covered with scales as it grows up. You can see the third eye on baby tuataras. Another amazing thing about a tuatara is how long it can hold its breath. It can go for one hour without breathing!

What about those babies? It takes them a long time to come into the world. Tuataras live to be 60 to 80 years old. They are not ready to mate until they are between 13 and 20 years old. Nine months after tuataras mate, the female lays eggs. Then, it takes at least one year for the eggs to hatch! The parents do not raise the babies. Baby tuataras have to take care of themselves on the islands of New Zealand where this animal lives. Rats like to eat tuatara eggs, and wild dogs eat the babies. That's one reason why this strange leftover from the age of dinosaurs might soon be gone forever.

Conversion

2 feet = 0.61 meters

Next Page

From the Days of the Dinosaurs

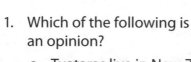

Answer the questions below.

1. Which of the following is an opinion?

   a. Tuataras live in New Zealand.
   b. These fascinating animals have many interesting traits.
   c. The tuatara lives a long time.
   d. Tuataras are not lizards.

2. Which of the following sentences is NOT true?

   a. A tuatara can hold its breath for one hour.
   b. The tuatara will eat its own kind.
   c. The tuatara is two inches long.
   d. One of the tuatara's enemies is the rat.

3. Read the following sentence from the story and answer the question.

   That's one reason why this strange leftover from the age of dinosaurs might soon be gone forever.

   Which of the following is a word that could replace *gone forever*?

   a. remote
   b. removed
   c. endangered
   d. extinct

4. What is the fastest amount of time between the mating of tuataras and the hatching of the baby tuataras?

   a. 9 months
   b. 10 months
   c. 12 months
   d. 21 months

5. Which of the following is NOT a feature of the tuatara?

   a. a third eye
   b. a second tail
   c. soft, loose skin
   d. teeth built into its jawbone

6. Do you think the tuatara makes a good baby-sitter? Why or why not? Write your answer in complete sentences.

   _____

   _____

   _____

   _____

   _____

   _____

Conversion

2 inches = 5.08 centimeters

Talk to Me

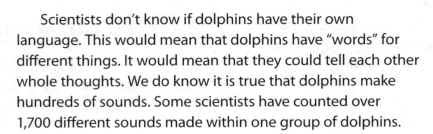

The **bottlenose dolphin** is a mammal, just like us. It breathes air like we do. It lives in family groups, called *pods*. But, can the dolphin also talk like we can?

Scientists don't know if dolphins have their own language. This would mean that dolphins have "words" for different things. It would mean that they could tell each other whole thoughts. We do know it is true that dolphins make hundreds of sounds. Some scientists have counted over 1,700 different sounds made within one group of dolphins.

Every bottlenose dolphin has a whistle that is its very own, like a name. Scientists call this a *signature whistle*. They think that it means something like this: "I am me, from this pod, and from this father and mother. Right now, I am happy (or sad, or scared)."

Dolphins use other sounds, too. They make a buzzing noise, a yell, a scream, and a noise that sounds like a motorbike. None of these sounds come from a dolphin's mouth. The dolphin uses its *blowhole* to make sounds. The blowhole is the hole on top of the dolphin's head.

Bottlenose dolphins "talk" in other ways, too. They use their bodies to speak. Dolphins kick with their tails. They roll their eyes, and they brush against other dolphins. Sometimes, two dolphins swim side by side and touch fins, as if they are holding hands.

Someday, scientists hope to know more about dolphin sounds. Then, they will be able to tell if the bottlenose dolphin has a real language or not.

Talk to Me

Answer the questions below.

1. Read the following sentences from the story and answer the question.

   Bottlenose dolphins "talk" in other ways, too. They use their bodies to speak.

   What is a possible name for this way of talking?
   a. motorbike speech
   b. body language
   c. eye contact
   d. swim talk

2. Which definition of *pod* is used in the story?
   a. common term for a group of office cubicles
   b. seeds and their covering
   c. a family group
   d. none of the above

3. Based on the story, what can you infer about the difference between animal sounds and a language?
   a. All animals that use cries have a language.
   b. Language means more than a series of calls or cries.
   c. Language means that each animal has its own call.
   d. Dolphins definitely have a language.

4. The story lists all of the following dolphin sounds EXCEPT—
   a. whistle
   b. yell
   c. motorbike sound
   d. bark

5.–8. Write T for true and F for false.

5. _____ Dolphins use their mouths to make their calls.

6. _____ Sometimes dolphins touch fins as they swim.

7. _____ Dolphins are fish.

8. _____ Scientists have heard over 17,000 different sounds between dolphins.

9. Describe one way that the bottlenose dolphin uses its body to talk. Write your answer in a complete sentence.

   _____

   _____

   _____

   _____

STOP

The King of the Frogs

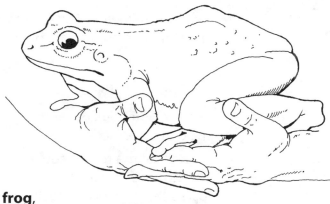

Frogs come in many sizes and colors. Some frogs are so bright in color that they look like toys! The smallest frog in the world is less than one-half inch long. That's smaller than most coins! This frog has a very big cousin in Africa. It is the **Goliath frog**, the biggest frog in the world.

The Goliath frog only lives in one place on the western coast of Africa. Its body is almost one foot long. When its legs are stretched out, they are about two feet long! The Goliath frog can weigh up to seven pounds. This frog is about as big as a house cat.

Explorers from Europe did not even know about this frog until 1906. It must have been a big shock to see a frog that size! Of course, people who live in the rain forest have known about the Goliath frog all along. They use the frog for both meat and medicine.

The brown-green Goliath frog lives in rivers and streams. It likes fast-moving water. It catches fish and shellfish to eat. When it is in danger, the frog can use its long back legs to jump 10 feet at a time.

Hunters in the area still trap the Goliath frog and so do hunters from other parts of the world. In the United States, people once had frog-jumping contests. Goliath frogs would be brought across the sea for these contests. Today, some people want Goliath frogs as pets. But, these huge frogs often die when they are taken away from their rain forest homes.

Conversions

0.5 inch = 1.27 centimeters
1 foot = 30.48 centimeters
2 feet = 60.96 centimeters
7 pounds = 3.18 kilograms
10 feet = 3.05 meters

Next Page

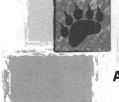

The King of the Frogs

Answer the questions below.

1. Read the following sentence from the story and answer the question.

   The smallest frog in the world is less than one-half inch long.

   Why do you think the author included this fact?
   a. so that the reader could learn more about small frogs
   b. so that the reader could learn about every frog in the world
   c. so that the reader can compare the smallest and biggest frogs
   d. so that the reader could learn about Goliath frogs

2. Which of the following sentences BEST sums up the main idea of the story?

   a. Goliath frogs are only one kind of frog in the world.
   b. The largest frog in the world is the Goliath frog from Africa.
   c. The Goliath frog is the size of a large house cat.
   d. The Goliath frog likes to live in fast-moving water.

3. Which of the following sentences is an opinion?

   a. It must have been a big shock to see a frog that size!
   b. The brown-green Goliath frog lives in rivers and streams.
   c. This frog is about as big as a house cat.
   d. Hunters in the area still trap the Goliath frog.

4. Why is the Goliath frog hunted and trapped?
   a. for food
   b. to be a pet
   c. for medicine
   d. all of the above

5. The Goliath frog eats _____

   _____ .

6. When it is in danger, the Goliath frog can jump _____ at a time.

7. When you add the length of the Goliath frog's body and legs, it is almost _____ feet long.

8. People once bought Goliath frogs to enter in _____ contests.

9. Do you think that the Goliath frog would make a good pet? Why or why not? Write your answer in complete sentences.

   _____

   _____

   _____

   _____

STOP

Wow! That's Fast!

The human heart beats about 72 times every minute. If you were a **hummingbird**, your heart would beat 17 times faster! When it is flying, a hummingbird's heart beats about 1,260 times every minute.

In fact, the hummingbird does almost everything fast. It can fly up to 60 miles per hour. Its wings beat 75 times every second. When a hummingbird flies by you, you can hardly see its wings. They are a blur.

All of this speed is found in the smallest bird in the world. Most hummingbirds are only about three inches long, and some are smaller. Hummingbird eggs are the size of green peas. These tiny birds are so small that they can be killed by a bee sting!

A hummingbird's nest is also tiny. It is only about two inches wide. The female hummingbird makes her nest from spiderwebs. Then, she puts moss on the sticky outside of the nest. This makes the nest hard for enemies to see.

The hummingbird has a long beak, but it has no sense of smell. It uses its eyes to find flowers. Then, it laps up the *nectar*, or sweet juice, from the flowers. It uses its long, split tongue to do this. The bird has to drink its body weight in nectar every day, or it will die. This is because it uses so much energy for flying. It also eats tiny bugs.

Long ago, people thought that hummingbirds did not have feet. They never saw a hummingbird *perch*, or sit. In fact, the hummingbird has to perch many times a day to save its energy. But, like everything else that this tiny, swift bird does, it perches so quickly that people might not see it.

Conversions

60 miles per hour = 96.56 kilometers per hour
3 inches = 7.62 centimeters
2 inches = 5.08 centimeters

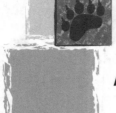

Wow! That's Fast!

Answer the questions below.

1. The title "Wow! That's Fast!" refers to—

   a. the human heartbeat
   b. the heartbeat of a hummingbird
   c. the life span of a hummingbird
   d. all of the above

2. Read the following sentence from the story and answer the question.

   But, like everything else that this tiny, swift bird does, it perches so quickly that people might not see it.

   What is a synonym for *swift*?

   a. cute
   b. thoughtful
   c. fast
   d. slow

3. Choose the BEST description of the hummingbird.

   a. a bird with a very fast heartbeat
   b. a bird that flies very fast
   c. a very fast bird that is the smallest bird in the world
   d. a bird that lays very small eggs

4. Why did people once think that the hummingbird did not have feet? Write your answer in a complete sentence.

   _____

   _____

5. Write three phrases from the story that tell about a hummingbird's size.

   a. _____

   b. _____

   c. _____

6. Why does a hummingbird have to eat so much every day?

   a. It needs to lay eggs.
   b. It needs to perch on branches.
   c. It needs to make nests from spiderwebs.
   d. It uses so much energy when it flies.

7. Circle the three phrases that BEST describe features of the hummingbird.

   fast wings   pea-sized eggs

   large feet   split tongue

   very still   short beak

STOP

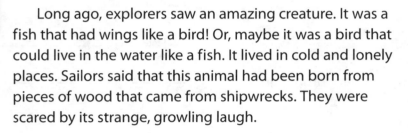

Is It a Bird? Is It a Fish?

Long ago, explorers saw an amazing creature. It was a fish that had wings like a bird! Or, maybe it was a bird that could live in the water like a fish. It lived in cold and lonely places. Sailors said that this animal had been born from pieces of wood that came from shipwrecks. They were scared by its strange, growling laugh.

Today, the **Atlantic puffin** is loved, not feared. Many puffins live near Iceland. This amazing seabird likes the cold water. A puffin can actually "fly" underwater! It uses its wings to help it dive deep into the sea. That's where it catches small fish to eat. The sailors from long ago thought that puffins were fish because they could stay underwater for so long. A puffin usually catches about 10 small fish during one dive. One scientist saw a puffin catch 62 little fish during a dive!

A puffin spends most of its life on the water. When it is not diving for food, it floats on the cold waves of the sea. When it is young, the puffin spends years at sea without ever coming to land.

The puffin does not always live in the sea. It lives on land when it is hatching and raising its chicks. The birds like rocky cliffs where they build burrows instead of nests. This gives them a place to lay eggs out of the cold wind and rain. On land, the puffin is not as graceful as it is in the water. It waddles out of its burrow and hops from rock to rock. The puffin can also fly. It flies fast—up to 55 miles per hour.

Make a prediction.

What do you think the author will write about next? Circle your answer.

the puffin's food   the puffin's home   the puffin's appearance

Conversion

55 miles per hour = 88.51 kilometers per hour

Answer the following questions based on what you read on page 31. Then, finish reading the story at the bottom of the page.

1. What is an antonym for *amazing*?

   a. awesome
   b. incredible
   c. boring
   d. different

2. Why does the author say that puffins can "fly" underwater?

   a. They are fish, not birds.
   b. They fly across the top of the water.
   c. They use their wings to help them dive deep in the water.
   d. They are good swimmers.

3. What is the one time in a puffin's life when it lives on land? Write your answer in a complete sentence.

   _____

   _____

   _____

4. Circle two phrases that BEST describe the puffin so far.

lives mostly at sea	bad swimmer
has three chicks at once	land bird
fierce fighter	good diver
flightless bird	scary bird

The puffin is about 10 inches tall with a stout body. Its feathers are black and white. Some people think puffins look like penguins. They are often called "sea parrots." This is because of their big, brightly colored beaks. The puffin has a large, curved beak that is striped in red, orange, black, and white. The puffin doesn't always look so flashy! Its beak changes from one season to the next. Every fall, the bright outer part of the beak is shed. The next spring, it grows back. The puffin also has orange webbed feet that look like duck feet. It has yellow eyes. The puffin's feet, eyes, and beak are bright spots of color in the vast waves of the sea where it lives.

Conversion

10 inches = 25.4 centimeters

Next Page

Is It a Bird? Is It a Fish?

Answer the questions below.

5. What did explorers and sailors think about the puffin long ago?

   a. It was both a bird and a fish.
   b. It was born from pieces of wood.
   c. It had a strange laugh.
   d. all of the above

6. Read the following sentence from the story and answer the question.

   Its beak changes from one season to the next.

   What happens to the puffin's beak?

   a. It falls off.
   b. The beak turns black after the puffin gets older.
   c. The puffin sheds the outer part of the beak every year.
   d. The puffin loses its beak when it fights.

7. Which of the following is an opinion?

   a. Puffins build burrows for their chicks.
   b. Puffins seem like strange, mythical creatures.
   c. Puffins live for years without coming to land.
   d. Puffins have bright orange feet.

8. Which of the following is a nickname for the puffin?

   a. driftwood bird
   b. penguin cousin
   c. duck-foot
   d. sea parrot

9. Which of the following is NOT a fact from the story?

   a. Puffins raise their chicks on land.
   b. A puffin can catch 10 fish at once.
   c. Puffins shed all of their feathers once a year.
   d. Puffins like rocky cliffs when they nest.

10. Write three details from the story that tell what a puffin looks like.

    a. _____

    _____

    b. _____

    _____

    c. _____

    _____

STOP

Peaceful Lives Overturned

People sometimes call the **koala** a "bear," but it is not. It has a pouch, like a kangaroo. A mother koala raises her baby in this pouch. When a baby koala is born, it is the size of a jelly bean! It is blind and has no ears. This tiny, pink baby lives in the pouch for months, drinking its mother's milk and growing bigger. When it is ready, it climbs out of the pouch and rides on its mother's back. That way, it can take its first look at the world. The baby, called a *joey*, lives with its mother until it is one year old.

When the joey grows up, it will spend much of its life sleeping and eating. It eats the leaves of the *eucalyptus tree*, a gum tree that grows in Australia. Koalas sleep about 16 hours every day. Each koala has a *territory*, or an area of land where it stays, roaming from tree to tree. Koalas look cute and cuddly, but they have sharp teeth and sharp claws. They use their claws for climbing trees. They do not fight very often. Today, the koala has a big problem that it cannot fight: humans.

As more people come to live in Australia, there is less land for the koala. Eucalyptus trees are being cut down. People build houses and ranches where koalas used to live. Roads built across koalas' territories are dangerous to the animals. Koalas are hard to see at night because of their gray fur. Cars sometimes hit koalas and kill them.

? **Make a prediction.**

What do you think the author will write about next?

_____

Answer the following questions based on what you read on page 34. Then, finish reading the story at the bottom of the page.

1. Read the following sentence from the story and answer the question.

   Roads built across koalas' territories are dangerous to the animals.

   What is an antonym for *dangerous*?
   a. hazardous
   b. difficult
   c. safe
   d. cautious

2. What is a baby koala called?

   a. a gummy
   b. a joey
   c. a kit
   d. a cub

3. About how big is a baby koala when it is first born?

   a. about 10 inches long
   b. about five inches long
   c. about one-fourth of an inch long
   d. about three-quarters of an inch long

Conversions

10 inches = 25.4 centimeters
5 inches = 12.7 centimeters
0.25 inch = 6.35 millimeters
0.75 inch = 1.91 centimeters

People have other things that are dangerous for koalas, like swimming pools and pet dogs. Koalas can swim for a short time. But, if they can't find a way to get out of a swimming pool, they can drown.

In Australia, many people do not keep their dogs on leashes. Dogs that chase koalas can kill them. Koalas cannot run fast enough to get away from dogs. Even a small nip from a dog means death for the koala because of certain germs.

What can be done for the koala? There are groups in Australia that are trying to help. They ask people not to cut down the trees in their backyards so that koalas will still have their homes. They tell people to keep their dogs inside at night. Another thing that people can do is put rope "ladders" for koalas in their swimming pools. A rope that hangs into the pool lets the koala climb out if it falls in. These are just a few of the things that can be done to help save koalas.

Next Page

Peaceful Lives Overturned

Answer the questions below.

4.–7. Write T for true and F for false.

4. _____ The koala is a type of bear.

5. _____ Koalas fight a lot.

6. _____ A joey stays in its mother's pouch until it is ready to leave her.

7. _____ The koala's biggest problem today is humans.

8. Read the following sentence from the story and answer the question.

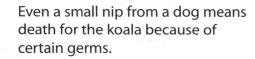

Even a small nip from a dog means death for the koala because of certain germs.

Which of the following phrases could be used in place of *means death for the koala*?

a. will kill a koala
b. means a spell is cast over the koala
c. means friendship for the koala
d. will bring pain to the koala

9. Which of the following does the koala eat?

a. eucalyptus tree berries
b. small birds
c. eucalyptus tree leaves
d. fish

10. List three things humans own that are dangerous to koalas.

a. _____

b. _____

c. _____

11. At the end of the story, the author writes about things that can be done to help the koala. Do these seem like small or big prices to pay in order to help keep this animal safe? Write your answer to this question.

I think _____

_____

because _____

_____

_____

_____ .

The Huge Hunter

If you were planning to hunt for food in the coldest place on Earth, how would you get ready? Probably by dressing very warmly! The **polar bear** is always "dressed" for its constant hunt for meat. The polar bear is covered with fur. Even the bottoms of its feet have fur on them. Its huge claws dig into the snow so that it can run without slipping. But, that's just the start of the polar bear's winter wear.

The polar bear has a thick layer of fat to keep it warm. This layer can be more than four inches thick. Its skin is black. Black is the best color to hold in the sun's warmth. Why doesn't the polar bear's white fur reflect the sun? Because even its fur is designed to keep the bear warm. Here's a surprise: the polar bear does not have white fur! The fur only looks white because of the sun's reflection. Polar bear fur is clear. Each hair is hollow. The sun travels through the fur and into the bear's black skin. This system is so good that the bear cannot be seen at all in infrared photos, pictures of things that give off heat. The bear's body traps heat well.

The polar bear hunts on the snow and in the water. The bear's feet are webbed to help it swim. It is a good diver and can see underwater. On the ice, the polar bear can be patient and still. The polar bear looks for an airhole that a seal has made in the ice. It can wait beside one of these holes for hours without moving. When the seal pokes its nose up to breathe, the bear grabs it and pulls it onto the ice. Seal meat makes up the largest part of the bear's diet. But, something is happening to make it harder for polar bears to hunt.

Make a prediction.

What do you think the author will write about next? Circle your answer.

polar bear hibernation   polar bear cubs   polar bear hunting problems

Conversion

4 inches = 10.16 centimeters

Next Page

Answer the following questions based on what you read on page 37. Then, finish reading the story at the bottom of the page.

1. Even the bottoms of the polar bear's

   _____ have fur on them.

2. The polar bear has a layer of fat on its body

   that can be _____ thick.

3. The polar bear's _____ is black

   to hold in the sun's heat.

4. The main thing that polar bears eat is

   _____.

5. The polar bear is ready to hunt on the ice and snow because of its—
   a. claws.
   b. thick fur.
   c. webbed feet.
   d. a. and b.

6. The polar bear's webbed feet help it to—
   a. run.
   b. swim.
   c. stay warm.
   d. all of the above

7.–8. Write T for true and F for false.

7. _____ The polar bear can swim, but it can't dive.

8. _____ The polar bear's skin helps to keep it warm.

Polar bears live in the Arctic. In fact, the word "arctic" comes from a Greek word meaning, "the country of the great bear." Scientists say that global warming is changing the polar bear's home and habits. The ice in the Arctic is getting thinner. It is also shrinking in size. What does this mean for the polar bear? The bear needs the ice to hunt seals, its main food. The big *ice packs*, or stretches of ice, are melting earlier in the year and refreezing later in the year. Without the ice to stand on, polar bears catch fewer seals and have less to eat. Fewer cubs are staying alive because the mother bears can't feed them enough. Scientists are watching to see if the huge hunters of the Arctic can survive as warming weather hurts their way of life.

Next Page ➡

The Huge Hunter

Answer the questions below.

9. Read the following sentence from the story and answer the question.

   Scientists are watching to see if the huge hunters of the Arctic can survive as warming weather hurts their way of life.

   Is this a fact or an opinion?

   _____

10. Which of the following BEST summarizes the story?

    a. Polar bears are "dressed" well for hunting in the cold.
    b. Polar bears are great hunters, but global warming might make it hard for them to survive.
    c. Polar bears are not built for the ice and snow, and that's why they are starting to die.
    d. Polar bears have a good body system for staying warm, and they are good hunters.

11. Why is global warming hurting the polar bear?

    a. The ice freezes earlier and melts later each year, making it harder for the polar bears to hunt.
    b. The ice melts earlier and freezes later each year, making it harder for the polar bears to hunt.
    c. The ice is melting so fast that the polar bears are drowning.
    d. The ice is melting too quickly for the polar bears to cross it.

12. What color is a polar bear's fur?

    a. white
    b. yellow
    c. black
    d. clear

13. Look at the chain of events below and answer the question.

A polar bear finds a seal's airhole.

    ↓

The polar bear stays very still.

    ↓

The polar bear grabs the seal.

    ↓

The polar bear pulls the seal onto the ice and eats it.

    Which step is missing?

    a. The polar bear dives into the water.
    b. The seal comes onto the ice.
    c. The seal pokes its nose through the airhole to breathe.
    d. The bear shares the seal meat with its family.

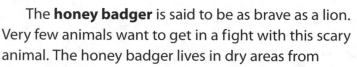

Badger with a Plan

The **honey badger** is said to be as brave as a lion. Very few animals want to get in a fight with this scary animal. The honey badger lives in dry areas from Africa to India. It can hunt in trees. It can dig up small animals or eggs underground. With sharp teeth and long claws, this animal will fight for any food. Scientists think that the honey badger's black, gray, and white fur is a warning. "Stay away!" says the skunk-striped fur of this easy-to-see animal.

How tough is the honey badger? For one thing, it can take on a snake. The honey badger loves snake meat. It will fight with dangerous snakes, like cobras, and eat them. Even when a snake bites a honey badger, it probably will not die. It will fall over and sleep for a few hours. Then, it will get up and start looking for food again.

The honey badger's digging skills help it hunt, too. Its claws are more than 1.5 inches long. It digs so fast that it can dig a hole the size of its own body in just two or three minutes. When it comes back up, it has a small animal, like a mouse or a hare, in its teeth. It is hard for even a fast animal to run away from this super digger.

The honey badger also climbs trees to find fruit. It uses its teeth to rip open melons that grow in the desert of South Africa. In other places, it looks for berries and even tasty roots. The honey badger likes sweet things. It likes honey best of all. But, to find honey, it has help.

Make a prediction.

What do you think the story will describe next?

_____

Conversion

1.5 inches = 3.81 centimeters

Answer the following questions based on what you read on page 40. Then, finish reading the story at the bottom of the page.

1. What is a *warning*?

   a. a sign of safety
   b. a notice of danger
   c. a dangerous element
   d. someone who is protected by another

2. Read the following sentence from the story and answer the question.

   The honey badger is said to be as brave as a lion.

   What kind of phrase is *as brave as a lion*?

   a. a metaphor
   b. alliteration
   c. slang
   d. a simile

3. Write three words or phrases that describe how the honey badger looks.

   a. _____

   _____

   b. _____

   _____

   c. _____

   _____

The honey badger has a honey-hunting friend. It is a bird called the **Greater Honeyguide**. This bird swoops over a honey badger. It calls to the badger. If the badger follows the honeyguide, the bird will lead it to a beehive. The badger uses its scent gland, like a skunk's, to stun the bees. Then, it claws into the hive to get to the honey. The honeyguide waits in a tree. After the badger has eaten, the honeyguide flies down. The bird eats the dead bees and the honeycomb that the badger has left for it.

Native hunters have told stories about seeing the badger and the bird. Some scientists think that this teamwork between the honey badger and the Greater Honeyguide is not real. Other scientists think that the honeyguide is changing. It may no longer help honey badgers to hunt. Even without the help of a bird, the fierce honey badger will keep going. Its brave, fighting spirit makes it first in line for food in the dry places where it lives.

Next Page

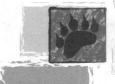

Badger with a Plan

Answer the questions below.

4. Finish this sentence to tell about the relationship between the honey badger and its helper.

   A bird called the _____

   _____

   helps the honey badger by

   _____

   _____ .

5. According to the story, in what two ways is a honey badger like a skunk?

   a. It eats snakes like a skunk and runs like a skunk.
   b. It has scent glands like a skunk and has webbed feet like a skunk's.
   c. It has scent glands like a skunk and is striped like a skunk.
   d. It has stripes like a skunk and can be a pet like a skunk.

6. Read the following sentence from the story and answer the question.

   When it comes back up, it has a small animal, like a mouse or a hare, in its teeth.

   Which animal is most like a *hare*?

   a. a squirrel
   b. a mouse
   c. a badger
   d. a rabbit

7. Which of the following groups of people has claimed to see the Greater Honeyguide helping the honey badger?

   a. scientists
   b. native hunters
   c. tourists
   d. none of the above

8. What does the Greater Honeyguide eat after the honey badger has finished eating?

   a. dead bees
   b. honey
   c. honeycomb
   d. a. and c.

9. Fill in the blanks to tell how the honey badger uses its body to get food.

   a. It uses its claws to _____

   _____ .

   b. It uses its sharp teeth to _____

   _____ .

   c. It uses its scent glands to _____

   _____ .

STOP

Batty for Fruit

Imagine you are walking at night. You hear a noise in the trees. Suddenly, you see something impossible. It's a fox with huge, pointed teeth. But, it's flying! And, its wings are six feet across!

This isn't a scene from a horror movie. This is a real-life animal, the **fruit bat**. You can find fruit bats on three continents: Asia, Africa, and Australia. There are 166 different kinds of fruit bats. These animals, with their huge wings and scary eyes, could be bad news for the animal kingdom if they ate meat. But, they don't. Fruit bats, as their name says, live mainly on fruit.

Fruit bats live in big groups called *camps*. Sometimes, a camp has over 1,000 bats in it. All of these bats hang upside down from tree branches during the day to sleep. When they wake up, they start "talking" to each other by screaming the same way that monkeys do. When night falls, the bats fly out to look for food. Fruit bats don't use echoes and sounds to find their way at night like other bats do. They see well and have a good sense of smell. When a bat finds a fruit tree, it uses its sharp teeth to rip open the fruit and eat. Then, it starts flying again. Its fur gets covered in pollen, and it pollinates the next tree where it lands. As the bat flies, it spits out seeds. These seeds become new trees. Even though they are a help to fruit trees, the bats are also pests. They can destroy an orchard by eating too much of the fruit. Farmers have a hard time keeping fruit bats away.

Let's meet some of the members of this big bat family.

Make a prediction.

What do you think the story will describe next?

_____

_____

Conversion

6 feet = 1.83 meters

Answer the following questions based on what you read on page 43. Then, finish reading the story at the bottom of the page.

1. The first part of the story describes all of the following EXCEPT—

    a. what fruit bats eat.
    b. where fruit bats live.
    c. what fruit bats look like.
    d. how baby fruit bats grow.

2. Which meaning of the word *camp* is used in the story?

    a. a place of temporary shelters, like tents
    b. a group of people sharing the same idea
    c. a colony of fruit bats
    d. to settle down

3. Why does the author compare seeing a fruit bat to a scene in a horror movie?

    a. Fruit bats have fox-like faces.
    b. The huge bats look like creatures from scary movies.
    c. There are many movies about fruit bats.
    d. Fruit bats are meat-eating hunters.

4. What is one adjective that describes the fruit bat?

    _____

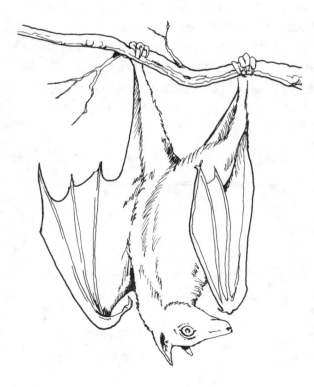

The **Angola fruit bat** looks the most like a fox. This big African bat has slanted eyes, red fur, and a soft, brown nose. The **Livingstone's fruit bat** has jet-black fur and bright orange eyes! This fruit bat lives on a few islands near Africa. There are only 1,200 of these bats left because people are cutting down the trees where they live. Farther north, the **Ryukyu flying fox** lives in Japan. Even though it has to put up with snow in the winter, this bat can live to be 30 years old. With its black and white fur, it almost looks like a flying skunk!

These fruit bats are very different from each other, but they share two things: their love of fruit and the dangers they face in the modern world. All fruit bats are in danger of dying out. Let's hope the "flying foxes" survive so that they can keep planting and pollinating fruit trees for many more years.

Next Page

Batty for Fruit

Answer the questions below.

5. Which of the following BEST summarizes the story?
   a. Fruit bats are scary.
   b. The Ryukyu flying fox lives in Japan.
   c. There are many different kinds of fruit bats, but they all share some features.
   d. Fruit bats are interesting animals.

6. Read the following sentence from the story and answer the question.

   Even though they are a help to fruit trees, the bats are also pests.

   What is an antonym for *pests*?
   a. enemies
   b. nuisances
   c. dangers
   d. helpers

7. Which fruit bat looks the most like a fox?
   a. Ryukyu flying fox
   b. Angola fruit bat
   c. Livingstone's fruit bat
   d. none of the above

8. Which of the following is NOT a feature of fruit bats?
   a. screaming like monkeys
   b. pollinating fruit trees
   c. using echoes to help it fly
   d. spitting out seeds that grow into new trees

9. The Livingstone's fruit bat—
   a. lives on a few islands near Africa.
   b. is dying out because people are cutting down too many trees.
   c. eats fruit.
   d. all of the above

10. Why does the author say that the Ryukyu flying fox looks like a flying skunk? Write your answer in a complete sentence.

   _____

   _____

   _____

   _____

   _____

STOP

A World of Danger

When a **green sea turtle** is born, its mother is not there to help it. It has to chip its way out of its egg with an *egg tooth*, a horn on the end of its beak. Then, it faces a big, scary world. Crabs, coyotes, and dogs are waiting on the beach to eat it for a snack. The baby turtle hides in the sand until night. Then, it scrambles to the sea. The little turtle has just made its first step in a long trip filled with danger.

The tiny baby starts to swim. To get away from the dangers of the beach, it swims for two or three days before it eats for the first time. It swims for one year or more before it crawls up on land again. In the sea, it may be eaten by tiger sharks or other fish. But, most of the dangers to the green sea turtle come from humans.

The little turtle might eat something that looks like a small fish. If it is a piece of plastic or another piece of trash floating in the sea, the turtle will die. Sometimes, turtles eat oil and die, too. Pollution in the sea is a problem for green sea turtles.

Turtles can also get trapped in fishing nets. Sometimes, they die before they can be set free again. Sea turtles are also hunted, both for their meat and for their shells. Even though there are laws against this, it still happens.

Only one in 1,000 baby sea turtles lives to become an adult. Those that do live go through many changes. Adult green sea turtles grow to be about 450 to 500 pounds. They stop eating jellyfish and other meat and eat only plants. And, they may plan a trip to go back home again.

Conversions

450 pounds = 204.12 kilograms
500 pounds = 226.8 kilograms

Next Page

Answer the following questions based on what you read on page 46. Then, finish reading the story at the bottom of the page.

1.–5. Write T for true and F for false.

1. _____ A baby green sea turtle stays with its mother for one year.

2. _____ The green sea turtle can die if it eats oil.

3. _____ One hundred out of 1,000 baby sea turtles become adults.

4. _____ The worst dangers that green sea turtles face are from humans.

5. _____ Green sea turtles are hunted for their shells.

6. Choose the phrase that BEST completes this sentence:

    The baby green sea turtle uses an _____ to get out of its shell.
    a. egg horn
    b. egg chipper
    c. egg tooth
    d. egg claw

7. The first part of the story tells about all of the following EXCEPT—
    a. why sea turtles go back home again.
    b. how sea turtles are born.
    c. what dangers sea turtles face in the sea.
    d. how much adult sea turtles weigh.

A female green sea turtle goes back to the beach where she was born. This is the only place where she will lay eggs. Even if it has been 40 years since she was a baby, she knows her way back home. She lays eggs in groups called *clutches*. Each clutch has 75 to 100 eggs in it. She buries her eggs in the sand. Then, the eggs are left to the weather. If the weather is warm, the baby turtles will be born female. If the weather is cool, the babies will be born male.

All of the turtles in a clutch are born at about the same time. They leave their safe eggs and start their journey. They swim thousands of miles. If they live, it will be at least 15 years before they head back to the beach where they were born.

Next Page

A World of Danger

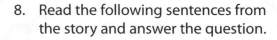

Answer the questions below.

8. Read the following sentences from the story and answer the question.

The baby turtle hides in the sand until night. Then, it scrambles to the sea.

Which of the following is an antonym for *scrambles*?

a. runs
b. plods
c. races
d. a. and c.

9. The green sea turtle is hunted for its—

a. meat.
b. egg tooth.
c. shell.
d. a. and c.

10. Out of 1,000 baby green sea turtles, how many will die before they become adults?

a. 99
b. 1
c. 100
d. 999

11. Which of the following will an adult green sea turtle NOT eat?

a. seaweed
b. algae
c. jellyfish
d. none of the above

12. A green sea turtle will only lay her eggs—

a. in clutches.
b. in the sand.
c. on the beach where she was born.
d. all of the above

13. What do you think might be another danger for the green sea turtle?

a. humans building homes and hotels on its home beach
b. dolphins that will eat it
c. coral reefs
d. losing its way in the sea

14. Finish this sentence:

Pollution is a problem for green sea

turtles because _____

_____

_____

_____

_____ .

Girls Rule!

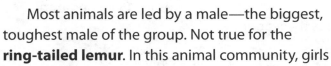

Most animals are led by a male—the biggest, toughest male of the group. Not true for the **ring-tailed lemur**. In this animal community, girls rule. Each group, or *troop*, of lemurs is led by a female. She has a special job in the group. She leads her troop through the rain forest every day as the lemurs hunt for food. Other females will fight the chief to try and win her special place.

Ring-tailed lemurs look like a cross between a monkey and a raccoon, but they are from the monkey family. You can't help but notice their tails. Most lemurs have bodies that are about 15 inches long, but their tails are two feet long! When lemurs follow their leader on the forest floor, they hold their black-ringed tails straight up in the air. They hook the ends of their tails. This makes the lemurs look like a line of question marks. When they rest in the trees, lemurs let their tails hang down like long, striped flags. Lemurs also have big, black rings around their yellow eyes. Their fur is light gray.

Females are so important to each lemur troop that they never leave the group. They are good mothers and carry their babies with them for a long time while they are growing. The babies are helpless. Sometimes, they die when they fall out of the tall trees while the lemurs are asleep. The female babies grow up and find a place in the troop. Males, though, roam and look for other troops to join.

Every day, the lemurs follow the same pattern.

Make a prediction.

What do you think the author will write about next?

_____

Conversions

15 inches = 38.1 centimeters
2 feet = 0.61 meters

Name _____ Date _____

Answer the following questions based on what you read on page 49. Then, finish reading the story at the bottom of the page.

1. Lemurs have _____ eyes.

2. A _____ lemur is the leader.

3. Lemur groups are called

    _____ .

4. Lemurs' _____ are

    about 15 inches long.

5. Only _____ lemurs will roam

    away from their home group.

6. Sometimes, baby lemurs die when they

    _____ .

The lemurs wake up high in the trees. They bask in the sun, which doesn't reach to the forest floor. They mew and purr at each other as they sit in small groups of friends and relatives. The female chief will decide when it is time to go walking in the forest. She climbs down the tree. All of the lemurs in the troop follow her. She takes the lead as the lemurs walk in a single line through the dangerous forest. The lowest-ranking male is at the end of the line. The lemurs call to each other to make sure everyone is safe.

The lemurs look for their food. They eat bugs and figs, flowers and bark, and the gum from some trees. Sometimes, a female will hit a male on the nose and take his food from him just to remind him that girls rule! The lemurs make a big circle through the forest and end up near the place where they started. They can see well in the dark. Like cats' eyes, lemurs' eyes glow in dim light. But, they do not like to be on the ground at night. When they get home, the lemurs climb back into their tall, safe tree to sleep.

Next Page →

Girls Rule!

Answer the questions below.

7. Read the following sentences from the story and answer the question.

   They hook the ends of their tails. This makes the lemurs look like a line of question marks.

   What kind of phrase is *like a line of question marks*?

   a. an idiom
   b. a simile
   c. a metaphor
   d. alliteration

8. Lemurs eat all of the following EXCEPT—

   a. bugs.
   b. flowers.
   c. mice.
   d. bark.

9. Which important job does the chief lemur have?

   a. She picks the males to stay in the group.
   b. She has babies so that the troop can survive.
   c. She leads all of the lemurs through the forest to look for food.
   d. She carries her baby with her while it is growing up.

10. Read the following sentence from the story and answer the question.

    Like cats' eyes, lemurs' eyes glow in dim light.

    What is another word for *dim* as it is used in this sentence?

    a. low
    b. bright
    c. clear
    d. blue

11. Which of the following is the MOST unusual feature of lemurs?

    a. They have rings around their eyes.
    b. They eat flowers.
    c. They are led by females.
    d. They mew and purr like cats.

12.–14. Write T for true and F for false.

12. _____ A female lemur will hit a male and take his food.

13. _____ Lemurs like to be on the ground at night.

14. _____ Lemur females leave the group to start a new troop.

Living Large, Lizard Style

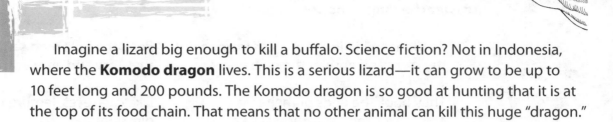

Imagine a lizard big enough to kill a buffalo. Science fiction? Not in Indonesia, where the **Komodo dragon** lives. This is a serious lizard—it can grow to be up to 10 feet long and 200 pounds. The Komodo dragon is so good at hunting that it is at the top of its food chain. That means that no other animal can kill this huge "dragon." It has no enemies.

The Komodo dragon has many features that help it hunt. Even though it has short, stubby legs, it can run fast. Sometimes, it doesn't have to. If a Komodo dragon bites another animal, the prey will start to die. That's because the Komodo dragon has *bacteria*, or poisonous germs, in its mouth. After biting its prey, the Komodo dragon walks slowly behind the animal until it drops to the ground. Then, it's time to eat.

This giant lizard also has a keen sense of smell. A Komodo dragon actually tastes the air with its forked tongue. It can use its tongue to smell animals up to five miles away. It has sharp claws and even sharper teeth. Its teeth have jagged edges and look like shark teeth. These teeth break off easily, but if they do, the Komodo dragon just grows more.

When it's not hunting, the Komodo dragon sleeps in its burrow or out in the hot sun. When it gets hungry, it will chase down a deer, a wild pig, or any other animal that gets in its way. It's a great life. The only real problems that the Komodo dragon faces are when it is young.

Make a prediction.

What do you think the author will write about next?

_____

Conversions

10 feet = 3.05 meters
200 pounds = 90.72 kilograms
5 miles = 8.05 kilometers

**Answer the following questions based on what you read on page 52.
Then, finish reading the story at the bottom of the page.**

1. Read the following sentence from the story and answer the question.

   The Komodo dragon is so good at hunting that it is at the top of its food chain.

   What does it mean for an animal to be *at the top of its food chain*?
   a. eaten by every other animal
   b. no enemies; the strongest animal
   c. not enough food to eat
   d. no food of the type the animal likes to eat

2. A Komodo dragon can be—
   a. 20 feet long and 200 pounds.
   b. 10 feet long and 100 pounds.
   c. 10 feet long and 400 pounds.
   d. 10 feet long and 200 pounds.

3. The first part of the story tells all of the following about the Komodo dragon EXCEPT—
   a. where it lives.
   b. what it eats.
   c. what happens to it when it is young.
   d. how it spends its days.

4. Finish this sentence:

   The Komodo dragon can poison its prey

   with the _____ in its mouth.

Conversions

10 feet = 3.05 meters
20 feet = 6.1 meters
100 pounds = 45.36 kilograms
200 pounds = 90.72 kilograms
400 pounds = 181.44 kilograms

The Komodo dragon has a special problem because it will eat its own kind. It will also eat Komodo dragon eggs. A mother has to work hard to hide her eggs. First, she digs a hole three feet deep. Then, she lays 30 eggs at one time. She quickly buries them so that they don't get eaten.

When the little Komodo dragons are born, they dig out of the sand and run as fast as they can for the trees. Adult Komodo dragons are too big and heavy to climb trees. So, the baby Komodo dragons live in the trees for at least two years. By never coming down, they don't become snacks for the adults. The babies live on insects, birds, and bird eggs. They only climb down from the trees when they, too, are ready to be fierce hunters and fighters.

Conversion

3 feet = 0.91 meter

Living Large, Lizard Style

Answer the questions below.

5. Look at the chain of events below and answer the question.

> Baby Komodo dragons hatch out of their eggs.

↓

> The babies dig out of the sand.

↓

> Baby Komodo dragons eat birds, bird eggs, and insects.

↓

> Baby Komodo dragons don't come down until they are ready.

Which step is missing?

a. The baby Komodo dragons are led to burrows by their mothers.
b. The baby Komodo dragons run to the trees.
c. The baby Komodo dragons lie on the sand to warm up.
d. The baby Komodo dragons dig burrows for themselves.

6.–9. Match each adjective to the part of the Komodo dragon's body that it describes.

6. _____stubby   a. teeth

7. _____jagged-edged   b. legs

8. _____forked   c. claws

9. _____sharp   d. tongue

10. How does the Komodo dragon find its prey?

a. It looks for it with its sharp eyes.
b. It smells it with its nose.
c. It tastes the air with its tongue.
d. It uses its night vision.

11. Read the following sentence from the story and answer the question.

This giant lizard also has a keen sense of smell.

What is another word for *keen* as it is used in this sentence?

a. cool
b. dull
c. excellent
d. wailing

12. Read the following sentence from the story and answer the question.

The Komodo dragon has a special problem because it will eat its own kind.

This means that Komodo dragons are—

a. cannibals.
b. kind-hearted.
c. competitive.
d. none of the above

STOP

Parakeets on the Run

If you were a wild bird, would you rather live in a tree or in a cage? Some parakeets in Chicago, Illinois, answered that question. They escaped from their owners. The birds built their own neighborhood in a part of Chicago called Hyde Park. All through the 1990s, students and scientists watched the birds and kept track of them. The most amazing thing about these parakeets is that they were able to survive at all.

Monk parakeets are green birds with gray breasts and yellow beaks. Some people call them Quaker parakeets or Quaker parrots. They are from South America, which has a warm climate. The birds are caught there and brought to places like the United States to be sold. Many people keep them as pets. They are friendly and easy to train. The birds are able to live in North America because they live indoors. But, the Hyde Park parakeets live outside in one of the coldest and windiest cities in the United States. How do they survive?

The escaped birds have built huge nests for themselves. These nests are made of hundreds of twigs woven together. The thick nests have small, round doorways. Many of the nests have more than one "apartment" inside. In fact, some of the Hyde Park parakeets have had squirrels move in with them! These squirrels have their own guest rooms in the warm, cozy nests. The parakeets don't seem to mind them at all.

In the summer, the Hyde Park parakeets eat buds, weeds, and fruit. They love crab apples, and there are many crab apple trees in Chicago. In the winter, they eat seeds at feeders like other birds do. They sit close together on telephone wires for warmth. And, their thick nests keep them from freezing at night. These Chicago parakeets have learned to live in the wild again. But, they aren't the only ones.

Next Page

Parakeets on the Run

Answer the following questions based on what you read on page 55.
Then, finish reading the story on the next page.

1. The first part of the story is MOSTLY about—
   a. parakeets in South America.
   b. a group of escaped parakeets in Hyde Park.
   c. how parakeets build nests.
   d. parakeets as pets.

2. Where is Hyde Park?
   a. North America
   b. Illinois
   c. Chicago
   d. all of the above

3. Why is it amazing that the Hyde Park parakeets live outdoors?
   a. Chicago is really too cold for them.
   b. Parakeets live indoors in South America.
   c. Parakeets die quickly.
   d. Parakeets would rather be pets.

4. What do Monk parakeets look like?
   a. gray birds with yellow breasts
   b. green birds with yellow breasts
   c. green birds with gray breasts
   d. yellow birds with green breasts

5. What is the MAIN way that parakeets survive in the cold weather of Hyde Park?
   a. They eat crab apples.
   b. They sit close together on telephone wires.
   c. They stay on the run so that their owners can't catch them.
   d. They build huge, thick nests out of twigs.

6. Read the following sentences from the story and answer the question.

   But, the Hyde Park parakeets live outside in one of the coldest and windiest cities in the United States. How do they survive?

   What is a synonym for *survive*?
   a. die
   b. prosper
   c. live
   d. quarrel

7. What do you think the author will write about next? Write your answer in a complete sentence.

   _____

   _____

   _____

Next Page

Finish reading "Parakeets on the Run" below. Then, answer the questions on page 58.

Other people across the United States have found parakeets on the run, too. Some of these birds live in warm places, like Atlanta, Georgia. But, other parakeets live in cold places. One group lives in Bridgeport, Connecticut. A scientist has an idea about them. He thinks that these birds were on their way to a pet shop. They were in a crate. The crate was dropped in an airport in New York City, New York. It broke, and the birds flew away to Long Island, New York. Later, they built nests in Connecticut, too. The Bridgeport parakeets build huge, thick nests like the ones built by the Hyde Park parakeets.

Some people are not so happy about these parakeets in the wild. In Chicago, some birds built a huge nest on a power line. It caused a fire. In Atlanta, people complained about a big, messy nest. The parakeets that built it were taken to a wildlife center. In St. Louis, Missouri, people are worried about how the birds will affect the land. They say if the birds move to the countryside, they will hurt crops.

Other people love the plucky birds. They think it is amazing that pet parakeets can live in the wild. They forget that many pet parakeets in North America were taken as babies from wild nests. Many people don't think of parakeets as wild birds. But, if these parakeets keep mating, people may someday view them as wild birds in North America, too.

Until then, if you see a flash of bright green in a tree one day, look up. You might see a huge, round nest of woven twigs. Maybe some escaped pets have made a wild home in your neighborhood, too.

Next Page

Parakeets on the Run

Answer the questions below.

8. The story talks about a scientist's idea about one group of parakeets. Look at the chain of events below and answer the question.

```
┌─────────────────────────────────────┐
│ parakeets caught in South America    │
└─────────────────────────────────────┘
                  ↓
┌─────────────────────────────────────┐
│ parakeets put in a crate             │
└─────────────────────────────────────┘
                  ↓
┌─────────────────────────────────────┐
│ crate dropped at an airport in       │
│ New York                             │
└─────────────────────────────────────┘
                  ↓
┌─────────────────────────────────────┐
│ parakeets built nests in Connecticut │
└─────────────────────────────────────┘
```

Which step is missing?

a. parakeets caught by pet store owner
b. parakeets flew to Long Island
c. parakeets had nest stolen by squirrel
d. parakeets taken to wildlife center

9. Which city is NOT mentioned in the story as a place where escaped parakeets live?

a. St. Louis, Missouri
b. Chicago, Illinois
c. Atlanta, Georgia
d. New Orleans, Louisiana

10. Read the following sentence from the story and answer the question.

Other people love the plucky birds.

What is a synonym for *plucky*?

a. brave
b. lucky
c. dreary
d. plodding

11. Which of the following is a reason that people do NOT like the parakeets?

a. A nest on a power line started a fire.
b. A nest fell down a chimney.
c. The parakeets might hurt crops.
d. a. and c.

12. According to the story, how can a squirrel live with the parakeets?

a. The squirrel kicks the parakeets out of the nest.
b. The squirrel has his own room inside the nest.
c. The squirrel and the parakeets sleep in the same room to keep warm.
d. The squirrel only lives in the nest during the daytime.

The Leopard That Went for Help

Billy Arjan Singh is a wildlife expert. He lives in India. At his home across the river from a big forest, he takes in orphans. These orphans have four legs and whiskers! Billy works with big cats, like leopards and tigers.

One orphan cub who grew up on Billy's farm was named Harriet. Billy raised this **leopard**, along with her sister Juliette. But, they were not pets. From the first day, Billy started to teach Harriet and her sister how to go back and live in the wild. He built tree platforms to teach them how to climb. He took them on walks in the forest. He showed them how to hunt. He watched them as they explored.

Harriet was careful never to hurt Billy. She even played with Billy's dog. She also learned her lessons about living in the wild. Harriet became wild herself. Finally, she was ready to go live in the forest. Billy rowed her across the river to the trees. She got out of the boat and went into the forest on her own. Billy kept track of Harriet for a while. He watched her from far away. He knew when Harriet went off to have cubs of her own. He thought he would never see her again.

He was wrong.

Floods came to the river and the forest. Harriet and her cubs were in danger. Even though she had lived in the wild for years, Harriet remembered the place where she had been safe as a cub. She took one of her cubs in her mouth. She dove into the floodwater. She swam to Billy's house, walked into the kitchen, and put her cub down on the floor.

Next Page

The Leopard That Went for Help

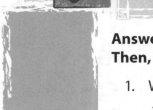

Answer the following questions based on what you read on page 59. Then, finish reading the story on the next page.

1. Who is Billy Arjan Singh?

   a. an Indian
   b. a wildlife expert
   c. a man who raises orphaned animals
   d. all of the above

2. Who was Harriet?

   a. a dog
   b. Billy's sister
   c. Billy's pet
   d. a leopard

3. What is an *orphan*?

   a. a person or animal without parents
   b. a leopard cub
   c. a person who has lost one parent
   d. an animal that lives in the wild

4. Why did Billy take Harriet to the forest and leave her there?

   a. He wanted to get rid of her.
   b. He wanted her to live in the wild where she belonged.
   c. He wanted her to live part of the time in the forest.
   d. all of the above

5.–9. Write T for true or F for false.

5. _____ Harriet didn't trust Billy anymore after she went to live in the wild.

6. _____ A huge forest fire put Harriet and her cubs in danger.

7. _____ Harriet had a sister named Juliette.

8. _____ Billy Singh lives in the forest.

9. _____ Billy built platforms in the trees to teach Harriet to climb.

10. What do you think the author will write about next? Write your answer in a complete sentence.

    _____

    _____

    _____

    _____

    _____

Next Page

Finish reading "The Leopard That Went for Help" below. Then, answer the questions on page 62.

Harriet went back to rescue her second cub and brought it to Billy's house, too. Billy's cook moved out and left the kitchen to the leopards! They lived there until the floodwaters started to go down.

Harriet watched the river every day. One day, she left her cubs with Billy so that he could take care of them. Harriet swam across the river and went to see her den. She decided that her den was safe again. She took the first cub across the river. But, the current in the river was strong. She had trouble swimming back to the farm again.

Harriet knew that if she swam across with the second cub, something bad might happen. So, Harriet the wild leopard asked for help. She took her cub in her mouth. She walked down to Billy's boat. She jumped in. Then, she stood there and waited for Billy to see her in the boat. When he did, he knew right away that Harriet was asking for a ride across the river.

Billy rowed Harriet and her cub across the river to the forest. She and her cubs went back to live in the wild again.

What is interesting about this story is that Harriet, who had lived as a wild animal, still trusted Billy. She remembered how to get to his farm. She knew that he would help keep her cubs out of danger during the flood. And, after the flood was over, she was able to understand that Billy's boat would be a safer way to travel back to her den with her cub.

Billy still lives on the farm near the forest. He still helps animals. He once said in an interview that Harriet was the love of his life. Her trust in Billy was like a bridge between wild animals and humans.

Next Page

The Leopard That Went for Help

Answer the questions below.

11. The story talks about all of the following EXCEPT—
    a. what happened to Harriet during the flood.
    b. where Harriet went to live after she left Billy's farm.
    c. how many cubs Harriet had.
    d. what happened to Harriet's sister.

12. Why do you think Harriet watched the river every day?
    a. She wanted to take her cubs back to the forest.
    b. She wanted to see if the water was safe again.
    c. She didn't like Billy anymore.
    d. a. and b.

13. What happened after Harriet took her first cub across the river?
    a. She had trouble swimming back to the farm.
    b. She did not go back for the second cub.
    c. She knew it wasn't safe to swim across the river again.
    d. a. and c.

14. How did Harriet ask Billy for help at the END of the story?
    a. She brought her cubs to his farm.
    b. She stood in his boat and waited for him to row across the river.
    c. She lived in his kitchen.
    d. She left her cubs in his care when she went to look at her den.

15. Based on Harriet's actions in the story, what can you infer about her?
    a. She never went back to Billy's farm again.
    b. She forgot about Billy once he had helped her.
    c. She might have gone back to the farm if she or her cubs were in danger again.
    d. none of the above

16. What is your favorite part of this story? Write your answer in a complete sentence.

    _____

    _____

    _____

    _____

    _____

STOP

Answer Key

Page 6
1. c.   2. a.
3. fast, horned
4. lioness, oryx, adopted it
   (or, took care of it)
5. d.   6. b.
7. spears

Page 8
1. d.   2. d.   3. b.
4. Bristles are sharp, little hairs.
5. Answers will vary but may
   include:
   a. light in weight
   b. hollow
   c. feels like a dry sponge
6. b.
7. friendly, loud, big-billed

Page 10
1. d.
2. A puggle is a baby platypus.
3. c.   4. F   5. T   6. T
7. F   8. F   9. b.
10. pads, bill, food

Page 12
1. b.   2. d.
3. baby-sitter (or, system)
4. Crocodiles
5. tongue
6. enemies
7. b.   8. d.   9. a.

Page 14
1. A female clown fish lays 300 to
   700 eggs at one time.
2. c.   3. T   4. F   5. F
6. T   7. F   8. d.
9. a. tentacles
   b. some enemies
   c. bait
10. The clown fish has bright
    colors and stripes like a clown.

Page 16
1. c.   2. d.   3. c.
4. b.   5. c.   6. c.
7. Answers will vary.

Page 18
1. a.   2. c.   3. b.
4. d.   5. d.
6. three years old
7. to keep the sun from
   blinding them
8. Answers will vary but may
   include: long legs, special
   pads on paws, large lungs,
   lightweight bones

Page 20
1. d.   2. a.   3. e.   4. b.
5. c.   6. c.   7. b.
8. a. save energy
   b. upside down
   c. large snakes and big birds
9. a. does not
   b. 20
   c. night
   d. claws

Page 22
1. Magellan
2. cat, monkey
3. mane
4. eagles
5. squirrel, tail
6. F   7. F   8. T
9. F   10. b.
11. Answers will vary.

Page 24
1. b.   2. c.   3. d.
4. d.   5. b.
6. Answers will vary, but will
   probably be "no" since
   tuataras sometimes eat
   petrel chicks.

Page 26
1. b.   2. c.   3. b.   4. d.
5. F   6. T   7. F   8. F
9. Answers will vary but may
   include: kick tail, roll eyes,
   swim side-by-side and touch
   fins with other dolphins,
   brush against other dolphins

Page 28
1. c.   2. b.   3. a.   4. d.
5. fish and shellfish
6. 10 feet
7. three
8. frog-jumping
9. Answers will vary.

Page 30
1. b.   2. c.   3. c.
4. No one ever saw it perch.
5. Answers will vary but may
   include:
   a. smallest bird in the world
   b. pea-sized eggs
   c. nest is only about two
      inches wide
6. d.
7. fast wings, pea-sized eggs,
   split tongue

Page 31
the puffin's appearance

Page 32
1. c.   2. c.
3. The puffin lives on land while
   it hatches and raises its chicks.
4. lives mostly at sea, good diver

Next Page

Page 33
5. d.   6. c.   7. b.
8. d.   9. c.
10. Answers will vary but may
    include:
    a. 10 inches tall with a
       stout body
    b. black and white feathers
    c. large, curved beak striped
       in red, orange, black,
       and white

Page 34
more dangers for the koala

Page 35
1. c.   2. b.   3. d.

Page 36
4. F   5. F   6. F
7. T   8. a.   9. c.
10. Answers will vary but may
    include:
    a. dogs
    b. cars
    c. swimming pools
11. Answers will vary.

Page 37
polar bear hunting problems

Page 38
1. feet
2. four inches
3. skin
4. seal meat
5. d.   6. b.   7. F   8. T

Page 39
9. fact
10. b.   11. b.   12. d.   13. c.

Page 40
who or what helps the honey
badger find honey

Page 41
1. b.   2. d.
3. Answers will vary but may
   include:
   a. gray, black, and white fur
      (or, like a skunk)
   b. sharp teeth
   c. long claws

Page 42
4. the Greater Honeyguide,
   leading it to a beehive
5. c.   6. d.   7. b.   8. d.
9. a. dig up animals
   b. rip open melons
   c. stun bees

Page 43
some members of the
fruit bat family

Page 44
1. d.   2. c.   3. b.
4. Answers will vary but
   may include: huge, scary,
   nocturnal, vegetarian

Page 45
5. c.   6. d.   7. b.
8. c.   9. d.
10. Answers will vary but may
    include: The Ryukyu flying fox
    looks like a flying skunk
    because it has black and
    white fur.

Page 47
1. F   2. T   3. F   4. T
5. T   6. c.   7. a.

Page 48
8. b.   9. d.   10. d.
11. c.   12. d.   13. a.
14. Answers will vary.

Page 49
the lemur's daily routine

Page 50
1. yellow
2. female
3. troops
4. bodies
5. male
6. fall from the trees

Page 51
7. b.   8. c.   9. c.   10. a.
11. c.   12. T   13. F   14. F

Page 52
dangers for young
Komodo dragons

Page 53
1. b.   2. d.   3. c.
4. bacteria (or, poisonous germs)

Page 54
5. b.   6. b.   7. a.   8. d.
9. c.   10. c.   11. c.   12. a.

Page 56
1. b.   2. d.   3. a.
4. c.   5. d.   6. c.
7. The author will write about
   other escaped parakeets or
   pets living in the wild.

Page 58
8. b.   9. d.   10. a.
11. d.   12. b.

Page 60
1. d.   2. d.   3. a.   4. b.
5. F   6. F   7. T   8. F
9. T
10. The story will tell more about
    the flood and its affect on
    Harriet and her cubs.

Page 62
11. d.   12. d.   13. d.
14. b.   15. c.
16. Answers will vary.